THE BATTLE *of* NEW ORLEANS

and Its Monument

THE BATTLE *of* NEW ORLEANS

and Its Monument

LEONARD V. HUBER

A Louisiana Landmarks Society Book

PELICAN PUBLISHING COMPANY
GRETNA 2012

Published by arrangement
with the
Louisiana Landmarks Society
by
Pelican Publishing Company, Inc., 2012

First printing, 1983
First Pelican edition, 2012

ISBN 9781589809857

Printed in the United States of America
Published by Pelican Publishing Company, Inc.
1000 Burmaster Street, Gretna, Louisiana 70053

THE BATTLE OF NEW ORLEANS
JANUARY 8, 1815

Major-General Andrew Jackson (1767-1845), hero of the Battle of New Orleans, from a painting by John Vanderlyn executed in 1819.

Battle of New Orleans:
January 8, 1815

The Battle of New Orleans was the last major battle of the War of 1812. This war, which had been going on for nearly a year and a half without any decisive military action, suddenly became alive when the British, after defeating Napoleon in April, 1814, were able to turn their mighty war machine toward the United States. An expenditionary force under Admiral Alexander Cochrane raided Washington and burned the White House and attacked Fort McHenry at Baltimore. Joining a fleet of troopships from England in Jamaica in the West Indies, Cochrane and General John Keane sailed for the Louisiana coast and arrived with fifty ships carrying one thousand guns on December 9, 1814.

The British decided not to sail up the river past Fort St. Philip, but approached the city from the rear, through Lake Borgne, a shallow arm of the Gulf of Mexico. On December 14, after a sharp engagement, British barges captured five small American gunboats guarding the water approaches to the city, thus laying the way open for invasion. The British made their way in small boats to the mouth of Bayou Bienvenu, the entrance to an unguarded route to New Orleans on the Mississippi River. During the night of December 22-23, they had advanced to a point just nine miles below New Orleans. Pushing upriver during the day of December 23, they spread over the Villeré, Lacoste, and de La Ronde plantations and made camp for the night.

Meanwhile, General Andrew Jackson, then commander of the military district that included Louisiana, had arrived in New Orleans on December 2, bringing with him his regulars and elements from the Tennessee militia. Jackson had hardly time to organize his forces when the British were on American soil; when he received news of the British

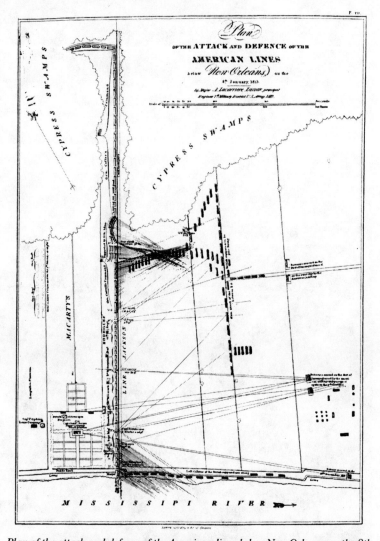

Plan of the attack and defense of the American lines below New Orleans on the 8th of January, 1815.

By Major A. Lacarriere Latour, Principal Engineer.
7th Military District, 1815.

The Battle of New Orleans, engraving by John Andrews.

From *Ballou's Pictorial Drawing Room Companion* (1850s).

approach he decided upon a very bold night of December 23, in their camp. Catching them off guard, he gave the leaders the impression that they were being met by a very formidable move. He struck the enemy on the force. Jackson withdrew his men to the Rodriguez Canal, a ditch about fifteen feet wide that separated the Chalmette and Macarty plantations. Along this ditch his men threw up a mile-long shoulder-high rampart, using mud, rails, fence posts, wooden kegs, and anything they could get their hands on. This rampart occupied a most fortunate position between the Mississippi River on one side and an almost impassable swamp on the other.

On Christmas Day, 1814, General Sir Edward M. Pakenham, brother-in-law of the Duke of Wellington, arrived to take command of the British forces. Pakenham ordered an attack on the Americans on December 28. His men began advancing in two columns, one near the river and the other near the swamp, through the stubble of the plantation cane fields.

The American sloop *Louisiana* came downriver and began firing into the nearest British column, and artillery fire from the American lines forced the column by the river to withdraw. The commander of the British column near the swamp, seeing that he had no support on his left, called off his attack.

On January 1, 1815, Pakenham ordered his artillery to try to silence the American guns and break through the rampart. The British had brought up heavy artillery from the fleet with incredible labor, and a battery was erected about seven hundred yards from the American line. Pakenham's forces began a terrific fire, accompanied by a shower of rockets that were designed to frighten the defenders. The American guns answered, and so great was their accuracy that by noon the British guns were completely silenced.

Fearing that further delay would demoralize his army, Pakenham made preparations for a head-on assault against

MACARTE'S, JACKSON'S HEAD-QUARTERS.[1]

At the time of Lossing's visit in 1861, the Major-General Andrew Jackson's headquarters in the Battle of New Orleans was still in existence. The plantation house of Edmond Macarty, it survived until 1896, when it burned.

From a sketch made in April, 1861 by Benson J. Lossing, from *Lossing's The Pictorial Field Book of the War of 1812.* New York. 1868.

the Americans, even though some of his junior officers thought that such an attack would fail.

In the half light of the early morning of January 8, Pakenham sent his forces in a frontal attack on the Americans. He had hoped to take advantage of the darkness to get his troops within a few yards of the American line without being seen, but a delay caused by one of his junior officers in forgetting to bring ladders and bundles of sticks to throw in the ditches to help scale the ramparts cost him the advantage. Pakenham, nevertheless, determined to proceed with the attack. General Samuel Gibbs attacked the American left and center with a brigade of three thousand men. As the

Jackson's visit to New Orleans.

A hero's welcome was given to General Jackson by the people of New Orleans.

From a woodcut in the Author's Collection.

British advanced across the open fields, the artillery fire from the American batteries quickly tore huge gaps in their ranks. The redcoated British troop quickly filled in where their comrades had fallen and continued their advance in measured time until they came within musket range. Then the crack shots from Tennessee and Kentucky, who made up this part of the line, opened up on them with their long rifles. This checked their advance and killed many, including their commander, General Gibbs.

On the British left along the river, General Keene divided his brigade. One force under Colonel Robert Rennie was sent against the extreme right of the American

12

General Andrew Jackson, in old age, drawn from life, silhouette by William H. Brown, lithograph by E. B. and E. C. Kellog, 1844.

line. Keene then took a regiment of Scottish Highlanders obliquely across the field to help General Gibbs. The regiment suffered frightful casualties from the galling fire of the batteries. Keene rallied the remainder of Gibbs's men, and again assaulted the American center. This time he was severely wounded, and as his attack on the right was failing, General Pakenham himself rode forward to rally his men for a third assault. In this action, Pakenham was shot and killed. Colonel Rennie's attack on the right was repulsed after fierce hand-to-hand combat. A British force across the river, successful at first, had to be recalled, and because of the bitter defeat suffered by their main force, General John Lambert, now commander in chief, ordered an end to hostilities. The casualties in this dreadful battle were 2,057 British, 71 Americans. Rarely had professional veteran soldiers been defeated in so one-sided a battle.

Some days later, far down the river at Fort St. Philip, the British sent four ships of war in an attempt to silence the batteries of the fort, and although they fired more than a thousand rounds, the fort never failed to respond. After ten days the British left. On the plains of Chalmette, the Americans discovered on January 19 that the enemy, leaving campfires burning, had stolen away, returned to their ships, and sailed off. Ironically, two weeks before the final Battle of New Orleans, on January 8, representatives of the United States and Great Britain had signed a treaty of peace at Ghent, Belgium, a fact not known by any of the participants in the battle.

The Battle of New Orleans and the American victory had a profound effect upon our history. It not only saved New Orleans from conquest by the British, and made the Mississippi an American river, but it opened the way for westward expansion. It increased our nation's prestige in the world, gave the young United States confidence in its military powers, and increased the national feeling of unity. It made a popular hero of Andrew Jackson, and did much to stamp the effects of frontier democracy on the American social and political order.

The Chalmette Monument

Twenty-four years had elapsed since the American victory at the Battle of New Orleans. In 1839 a group which called themselves the Young Men's Jackson Committee was formed to try to raise the money to build a monument. A wordy constitution was adopted, but apparently the Monument Committee died aborning.

For the twenty-fifth anniversary of the Battle of New Orleans a committee of citizens invited the former President of the United States and the hero of the famous battle to come to New Orleans. Elaborate preparations were made to celebrate the event and to fete "Old Hickory." The white-haired General arrived aboard the steamer Vicksburg, appropriately, on January 8, 1840 and was met by leading citizens and the military. A parade through Canal Street to the Place d'Armes was viewed by thousands of the city's inhabitants.

On the very same day, at the battlefield, a huge crowd gathered. They had been told that there would be a cornerstone laying for a battle monument and that General Jackson would be there in person. To their great disappointment, General Jackson did not arrive and there was no cornerstone laying. There had been confusion in making arrangements! Next day *The Picayune* reported:

[the enormous crowd came in] steamboats, towboats, railroad cars, coaches, cabs, cabriolets, hacks, horses, wagons, sand carts, go carts, hand carts, drays, dugouts, in short every description of land carriage and water craft. There were big bugs in buggies, and little niggers on foot, in short all orders were there, marching in most admired disorder to the battlefield and like 'him of France' when they got there they right-faced home again . . . there was no Jackson and no cornerstone.

General Jackson, accompanied by about a hundred well-wishers did visit the battlefield two days later on January 10, a dreary winter day.

John Smith Kendall, in his *History of New Orleans* continues the story of the missing cornerstone for the Battlefield Monument:

A day after the departure of General Jackson (he left on January 13) it was ascertained that the Battleground Committee had chartered a steamboat and that a piece of granite with the inscription 'Eighth of January, 1815' cut upon it was put aboard and taken to the scene of General Jackson's victory.

Then follows a semi-comical paragraph which Professor Kendall states appeared in *The Louisianian:*

. . . the stone was then placed, fixed or laid in some spot, position or situation, we don't know which, or what, by three or four gentlemen, all there were on board. Whatever the object was, whether they were hoaxed themselves, or tried to hoax others, is more than we can say. Time will tell the story.

Professor Kendall wrathfully concludes:

It appears that there was no ceremony whatever in connection with the laying of the cornerstone of a monument intended to commemorate one of the greatest battles in history; and that the ill luck with which it was begun, then followed it for more than seventy years, during which time it remained a rudely truncated shaft and was then tardily completed only through the action of the United States Government.

If a stone was brought to Chalmette and buried in the earth, as was the cornerstone for the Jackson statue, it was never found. Apparently there was no cornerstone laying when the monument was being constructed fifteen years later; if there was, the event went unnoticed in the local newspapers. The cornerstone in the Place d' Armes was laid in ceremonies in which General Jackson participated on the day he left New Orleans, never to return (January 13, 1840).

In 1845, Major General Andrew Jackson died and in New Orleans, although a gigantic parade preceded obsequies in the Public Square, no plans for a monument or monuments were mentioned.

It was not until 1851, eleven years after the General had laid the cornerstone, that a meeting was called and a substantial organization, the Jackson Monument Association, came into being. The original members were: the Governor, Joseph Walker; The Lieutenant Governor, General Jean Baptiste Plauché; the Secretary of State, Charles Gayarré; the Mayor of New Orleans, A. D. Crossman; Recorder of Municipality No. 1, Joseph Genois, Recorder of Municipality No. 2, James H. Caldwell; and Recorder of Municipality No. 3, Pierre Seuzeneau. (This was at the time that the three municipalities each had its own governing body headed by a Council and Recorder.) There were patriotic speeches by Alexander Dimitry and General Plauché and resolutions were passed to enable the group to solicit money for the erection of the monument and to ask the State for help if it was needed.

At the end of six months the members of the Association had only collected $4,140.00 and they realized that there would have to be much help from the State if the projects could be started. An appeal to the Legislature brought official recognition to the Association and an appropriation of $10,000 for the erection of the Jackson statue in Jackson Square and $5,000 to acquire a site for a battlefield monument, the latter, a subject which apparently previously had not been on the Association's agenda. (Act of February 29, 1852.)

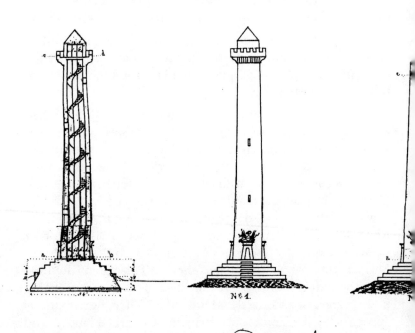

Nº 1.

Nº 2. Accepted by the Jackson Monument Associa
on the 30ᵗʰ May 1855/-

Signed— J B Blanchard
A.D. Crossman
J. Curris
James H Caldwell
P. Sergeant

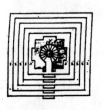

Horizontal Section.
through a.b.

To the Commissioners
of the Jackson Monument Association.
New Orleans. March 19ᵗʰ 1855

Respectfully
(Signed) Newton Richard
J.

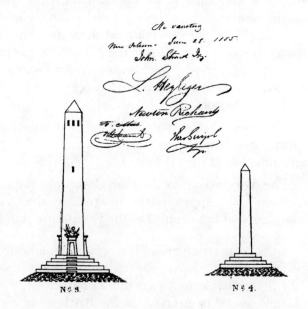

Horizontal Section
through c-d.

Drawings of the proposed Battlefield Monument showing design variations. The original is in the Orleans Parish Notarial Archives, as is the specification for building the monument.

When news of the $5,000 appropriation became known, the owner of the battlefield, one E. Villavaso wanted the full amount for his land. This the Association thought exorbitant and the *Picayune's* editor suggested that the land be taken by eminent domain, but Villavaso apparently sold his land; when the Act of Sale was passed on February 14, 1855, the owner from whom it was purchased was listed as M. Bachelot, but the price remained the same — $5,000.00.

Three years had passed from the time that the Legislature appropriated the $5,000.00 to buy the site and the consummation of the sale!

The Association was then faced with making a decision to choose an appropriate design for the battlefield monument and in its report to the Legislature stated:

> . . . the Association are of the opinion that in order to carry out in a proper manner the manifest design of the State, that a shaft or column of at least 120 feet in height should be erected on the Battle Field, so as to form a conspicuous point of attraction and elevation which could be discerned at a distance of many miles and thus strike the beholder and always bring to mind the great event that occurred on that memorable spot.

The Association warned the Legislature that to erect such a majestic monument would require a larger means than the Association has now at its command, and it must remain with the Legislature to determine to what extent the State is willing to embark in the furtherance of this undertaking.

On October 19, 1854, the members of the Association, consisting of General J. B. Plauché, Pierre Seuzeneau, A. D. Crossman, J. H. Caldwell and Joseph Genois, accompanied by Newton Richards, designer of the monument, John Stroud, contractor, and J. A. D'Hemecourt, City Surveyor, visited the site of the battle. After due consultation, they fixed the site of the monument at four arpents (767 feet) from the river along Jackson's old battle line.

In April, 1855 the Association examined several plans to erect the monument. One of these was to build a "bronzed cast-iron structure 75 feet high" which was proposed by the firm of Cook Brothers, lessees of the Belleville Iron Works in Algiers. This was rejected. The local stone dealers Newton Richards and John Stroud and Company submitted four designs, all drawn to scale on a single sheet. All of the designs were of Egyptian obelisks. The first shaft slightly taller than the second, featured a crenellated parapet. The second design was similar to the first, except that there was no parapet. Including a series of steps at the base, it was to be 150 feet high. Its only ornaments were four Egyptian-type doorways, only one of which was to be functional. Design numbers three and four were respectively to be three quarters and one half the size of the second design.

After considerable discussion, the members of the Association selected design number two.

Newton Richards, who had designed the monument, was born in New Hampshire in 1805. He learned his trade in Boston and in a succession of moves from New York and Philadelphia he came to New Orleans at the age of 26 and founded his stone business. A man of considerable energy, a local newspaper reported that he had "infused new life into our mechanics, builders and property owners." Richards was a good friend of Mayor Crossman and he consistently worked with the Monument Association in their efforts to erect the Jackson Square statue and the battlefield monument.

In Newton Richards' time (the early Victorian age) many architects were designing buildings in the classical Graeco-Roman, the Gothic and occasionally, in Egyptian styles. Of the three types, the Egyptian was better adapted to monuments than houses and Richards wisely chose the clean, spirelike obelisk as most suitable. Egyptian obelisks were usually of monolithic pieces of granite and their lofty,

Abdiel Daily Crossman (1805-1859) three times mayor of New Orleans, was chairman of the Jackson Monument Association (1851-1856). Although successful in the erection of the equestrian statue of Major-General Andrew Jackson in Jackson Square, circumstances thwarted the completion of the Chalmette Monument.

From a portrait in the Louisiana Division
of the New Orleans Public Library.

General Jean Baptiste Plauché (1785-1860) who served under Major-General Andrew Jackson at the Battle of New Orleans, commanding a battalion of volunteers. He was a memer of the Jackson Monument Association and was present when the site for monument was selected.

From a portrait in *History of Louisiana*
by Alcee Fortier.

Charles Gayarré (1805-1895) a historian and a member of the Jackson Monument Commission was Secretary of State when appointed.

From a portrait of Gayarré as a young man
by Jules Lion (1830s)
Courtesy the Historic New Orleans Collection.

Newton Richards (1805-1874) who designed the original monument. Richards, a successful New Orleans stone dealer also designed and erected the pedestal for the equestrian statue of Major-General Andrew Jackson in Jackson Square. He, in partnership with John Stroud, another stone dealer, erected the foundation and lower part of the Chalmette Monument.

From a portrait in the Louisiana Division
of the New Orleans Public Library.

imposing appearance had so impressed later Europeans that they patiently removed them from Egypt and laboriously re-erected them in such cities as Rome, Paris, London and Istanbul.

On May 30, 1855 the Association finally adopted, by the unanimous vote, the joint plan of Newton Richards and John Stroud and Co., for a marble shaft 150 feet high, 16 feet 8 inches at the base[1] above the founda tion and 12 feet 6 inches at the apex.[2]

The Association then advertised for bids and since the only bidders were Richards and Stroud, a contract to erect a monument for the sum of $57,000.00 was signed before Theodore Guyol, Notary Public on August 30, 1855 and work commenced. Payments for the work were scheduled:

1st	When the excavation is made and the timber for the foundation laid[3]	$1,000
2nd	When the brick work of the foundation is built from bottom, six feet high	3,900
3rd	When the brick work of the foundation is built to its height, ready to commence the shaft upon	3,900
4th	When the shaft of the monument is built up to the height of at least fourteen feet, frontices, cornices, and stairway included	5,000
5th	For the next two sections of fourteen feet in height, $4,000 each	8,000
6th	For the next six successive sections of fourteen feet in height, $4,500 each	27,000
7th	When the last section, of sixteen feet in height which completes the work, and the doors, steps and everything is finished, the balance, viz...	8,200
		Total $57,000

By February, 1856 the foundation had been dug to a depth of 7½ feet, the underlaying timber placed and more than 400,000 bricks had been laid to bring the foundation to the height needed to receive the superstructure:

> The first three payments, amounting to $8,800 are due, and have been accordingly made. The builders are now about to contract for the marble and when it arrives here, they will push forward the work as rapidly as the safety of the structure will admit.

The Jackson Monument Association was entrusted with the joint projects of building the equestrian statue of the General in Jackson Square and of constructing the battle-field monument. On June 17, 1854, $15,000.00 had been received by the Association to start the battlefield obelisk; this was included in a grand total of $59,604.00 for both monuments. The equestrian statue cost $33,153.00 and expenditures for the Chalmette monument totaled $14,298.00 by the time that the Jackson statue in the Square was dedicated (February, 1856). This left a balance of $12,153.00 to complete the obelisk, a sum far too short to complete that work. Unfortunately, after its report to the Legislature in 1856, the Association apparently did not make official reports, for none have been found in the archives of the succeeding years, and we only get glimpses of further construction at Chalmette.

[1] Alfred F. Theard, the engineer who completed the monument many years later, wrote: "The design selected, while less elaborate and expensive than the most costly, was, undoubtedly, in my opinion, the most appropriate and most beautiful."

[2] The monument was actually constructed with the base measuring 14 feet 2 inches square.

[3] Before the advent of foundations of poured reinforced concrete, 19th century Louisiana builders of heavy structures would place a grillage of timbers at the bottom of the excavation and on this construct a brick foundation. The Chalmette monument rests on two layers of 8" thick timbers, the top layer laid at right angles to the lower one and spiked together. (A similar grillage of stout timbers is under the foundation of the New Orleans United States Custom House.) In 1907, when engineer Theard examined the foundation, he found the timbers "in a perfect condition" and in 1983 they were still functioning.

On May 11, 1856, a few months after the dedication of the Jackson statue in Jackson Square, the *Daily Picayune* reported:

> Erection of the monumental obelisk on the Chalmette battle plains was being rapidly prosecuted; there was material on the ground for about sixty feet of the intended 150-foot shaft of white marble . . .

The State, the press reported, had appropriated another $15,000.00 in 1857 and by February, 1859 the *Daily Picayune* complained that the appropriation was nearly exhausted:

> With $3,100.00 available and $31,000.00 needed, Chalmette Battle Ground monument commissioners were suggesting that more ground was available than was required and that part be sold to pay for laying out the grounds and making enclosures.

In 1906 George Stroud, son of one of the original contractors who had in his possession documents concerning the erection of the monument, told a reporter for the *Picayune:*

> The work . . . was suspended [probably in 1856] for lack of funds, but by order of the [Monument] Association . . . the contractors were notified April 2, 1857, to resume their work, coupled with the statement that the Association had sufficient funds at its disposal to build the monument up to fifty-six feet, at which time the work was stopped, and the payment then due was made March 2, 1859.

The author hazards a conjecture that the deaths of several members of the Monument Association may have been one of the causes why the completion of the monument was not vigorously carried on. Governor Walker, who had been greatly interested in the project died during its early

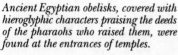

Ancient Egyptian obelisks, covered with hieroglyphic characters praising the deeds of the pharaohs who raised them, were found at the entrances of temples.

Author's Collection.

Benson Lossing, whose well-done delineations were made in Louisiana in 1861, drew this sketch of how he visualized the Chalmette Monument would look upon completion. The Monument, of course, eventually reached only two-thirds of Lossing's imaginative drawing.

From a sketch made in April, 1861 by Benson J. Lossing, from *Lossing's The Pictorial Field Book of the War of 1812.* New York. 1868

days, 1855; Pierre Seuzeneau in 1858; Chairman Crossman died at 54 in 1859; General Plauché, the next year, 1860; and James Caldwell in 1863.

The builders ceased work after the shaft itself was 56 feet 10 inches above the line at which the top of the step would meet it; this step or base, if completed, was about 12 feet 6 inches above the natural surface. (Total height above ground level — 69 feet 4 inches)

The building was temporarily topped off with a pyramidal-shaped wooden roof. This is shown on sketches made in April, 1860 by Benson J. Lossing and in 1873 by J. Wells Champney (see illustration on pages 23 and 24). This roof must have failed as photographs of the monument taken about 1900 show it with a flat roof.

For nearly half a century, the unfinished stump of the Chalmette monument stood on the Chalmette plain as a painful reminder of the State's failure to complete it. It was during much of this fateful period that Louisiana was being Reconstructed with a Federal military occupation in New Orleans that did not end until 1877.

In 1888 the Louisiana Legislature, hoping to get rid of the white elephant at the battlefield

passed an act agreeing to cede . . . the property to the Federal Government. Nothing, however, was done by Congress to complete the Monument, although the U.S. Government was in . . . possession of the grounds and monument from 1888 to 1893.

In August, 1890 a disgusted visitor to the monument wrote:

The approach from the river is through a narrow lane, so grown up in weeds and underbrush that even the narrow foot path is almost impassable, for ladies by reason of this growth, reaching eight or ten feet in height. The cultivated field which formerly left a

*The Monument on the Chalmette Battlefield (1873) from a sketch
by J. Wells Champney.*

From *The Great South* by Edward King.

The incomplete Chalmette Monument is seen in this sketch showing the remains of Rodriguez's Canal which was used by the Americans as a fosse or defensive ditch before their fortified lines in the Battle of New Orleans.

From a sketch made in April, 1861 by Benson J. Lossing, from *Lossing's The Pictorial Field Book of the War of 1812*. New York. 1868.

Chalmette's Plantation

In April, 1861, Benson J. Lossing made this sketch "from the foot of the shaft of the unfinished monument near Jackson's Headquarters and the line of intrenchments. This shows the principal field on which the battles of December and January, 1815 were fought. The plain is dead level."

From *The Pictorial Field Book of the War of 1812*. New York, N.Y. 1868.

Weeds 10 feet high around the base of the neglected monument are shown in this photograph, which was made in the 1890s.

reasonable open space about the base of the monument has been extended untilthe fences are now within twenty-five feet or more and the entire enclosure surrounding the monument is filled with weeds and rank vegetation eight or ten feet high and without even a foot path by which the structure can be approached (see illustration, page 31).

Three years later, things were about to change. A group of patriotic women organized as the Louisiana Society United States Daughters 1776 and 1812. Mrs. Edwin X. de Verges, their Historian, wrote:

Some time in the year 1893, a letter was published in one of the local newspapers, calling attention to the neglected condition of the Chalmette battleground and the unfinished monument. It was then that the United States Daughters of 1776 and 1812 conceived the idea to take up this work as their special privilege, believing that this society should be the proper guardian of the battle ground upon which had raged one of the most valiant conflicts in American history.

The group was incorporated in 1894 and the State placed the monument in its care.

Leaders in the Society were Mrs. J. W. Railey, Mrs. R. G. Hadden, Mrs. Felicité Gayoso Tennent, Mrs. Lelia M. Harper, Mrs. V. A. Fowler, Miss Lelia Forman, Mrs. George A. Rice and Mrs. Dora R. Miller. The State gave the women two appropriations of $1,000.00

and with this and the meager revenue derived from the sale of pecans, wood and the rental of pastures, built a keeper's lodge, cleared and drained the grounds, placed an iron fence and gate across the front, repaired old fences and put up new ones where necessary, built a mound for the monument, replaced twenty- one iron steps inside and placed a temporary top until such time as they could complete the Chalmette Monument.

By 1896 the group was sufficiently organized to attempt to do something to complete the monument. The architects Favrot & Livaudais prepared plans and specifications and received three bids for the work. These ranged from $6,800 to $7,282. Architect Livaudais then raised the question "Where was the money to come from?" Minutes of the Daughters succinctly state "The bids were not satisfactory."

In 1902, the State was asked by the Society to request the Federal Government to take over the monument and complete it within 5 years and return it to them. For the next several years, apparently no action was taken in Congress.

In 1906, at the urgent request of one of his friends and one of the ladies of the United States Daughters of 1776 and 1812, Alfred F. Theard, a civil engineer and a member of the Louisiana Engineering Society made an examination of the condition of the unfinished Chalmette monument. He wrote:

> I studied closely the conditions under which the work had been planned and partly executed, and thereafter submitted a written report covering the result of my investigation and making some suggestions as to the continuance of the work.

Theard's report so enthused the Daughters that they took it to Washington, appeared before a Congressional committee and finally in 1907, secured an appropriation of $25,000.00[1] that made the work possible. As a further result, Theard was employed by the War Department as the project engineer. Then, he wrote:

> [I] commenced a thorough investigation of the actual conditions at the monument. Considering it absolutely necessary from a professional standpoint, I

---

[1] $40,00.00 more was eventually spent at Chalmette by the Federal Government according to George C. H. Kernion (speech of November 16, 1933).

had at my own expense excavations made, and exposed the entire west side of the foundations down to the bottom. I desired to ascertain the exact condition of these foundations before attempting to increase the load then carried.

Finding the foundations in good condition, except for the first layers of bricks near the top, Theard made his calculations:

Reckoning 108 lb. per cubic feet of masonry and 50 lb. per cubic feet of timber, I figured that the foundation carried a load of nearly 2,000 tons or about 1,350 lbs. to the square foot, exclusive of the wedge of dirt which formed the mound. I estimated that I would add approximately not over 200 lbs. per square foot to the load, and I concluded that this was perfectly safe under the conditions found. The total load actually carried is 4,375,000 lbs. or very nearly 1,500 lbs. per square foot.

The monument could be increased in height, but not to the 150 feet figure that was called for in Richards' original design. The completed monument, Theard wrote, would only be about 100 feet high. From a design standpoint, this was unfortunate since the proportions of obelisk design call for a height about nine or ten times its width at the base (The Washington monument in the Capital is a good example of obelisk proportion.)

The contract for the completion of the monument was awarded to Captain Milton P. Doullut.* A copy of this contract has not been found; neither has a copy of the agreement that Doullut made with Victor Huber, a monumental contractor, to face the monument with marble. Photographs exist showing the monument under construction and Huber, with

* Captain Doullut also built the landmark "Steamboat Houses" on Egania Street in New Orleans.

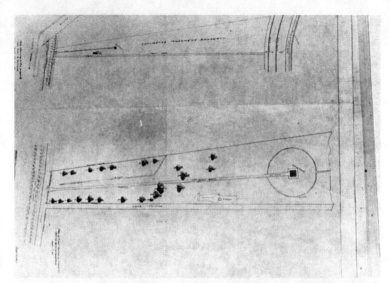

Until the building of the Chalmette Slip which interrupted the River Road, the main entrance to the monument was by a tree-lined shell path, a plan of which is shown here. (The door of the monument faces the river.) The entrance road from Highway 68 was a much later addition.

From a plan by Alfred F. Theard (1907)
Courtesy The National Park Service.

A 160-6 Chalmette Monument New Orleans, La

The unfinished Chalmette Monument as it appeared about 1905.

From a postcard printed in Germany.
From the collection of the Louisiana
State Museum.

Alfred F. Theard (1866-1939), Civil Engineer who designed and supervised the completion of the Chalmette Monument. Most of his professional life was spent solving the intricate problems of drainage in his native city. At his death, he was Superintendent of the Sewerage and Water Board of New Orleans.

Portrait courtesy Louisiana Department
Howard-Tilton Memorial Library
Tulane University.

his twelve marble cutters and setters at the job. One of the author's earliest memories is of a trip to the site with his father during construction in 1908.

The marble used in the original structure had come from a quarry in Tuckahoe, West Chester, New York. The material had been used in a number of pre-Civil War buildings in New Orleans among them the facade of Gallier Hall (Old City Hall). But the quarry had been closed and Huber was forced to find Tuckahoe marble that had come from former structures. At any rate, there must have been enough around in 1908 to permit the contractor to match the monument's lower part. The steps around the base of the monument were constructed of white Georgia marble.

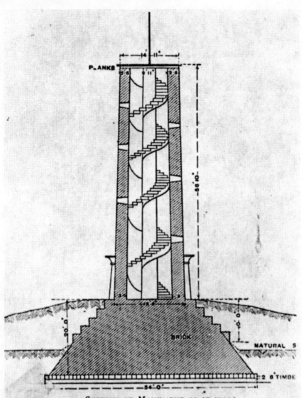

SECTION OF MONUMENT AS IT WAS.

*Section of the Monument showing
foundation as it was in 1907.*
From a drawing by Alfred F. Thread,
Engineer in charge (1907).

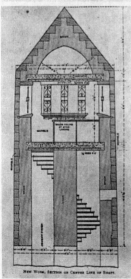

The New Section on center line of Shaft.
From a drawing by Alfred F. Theard,
Engineer in charge (1907).

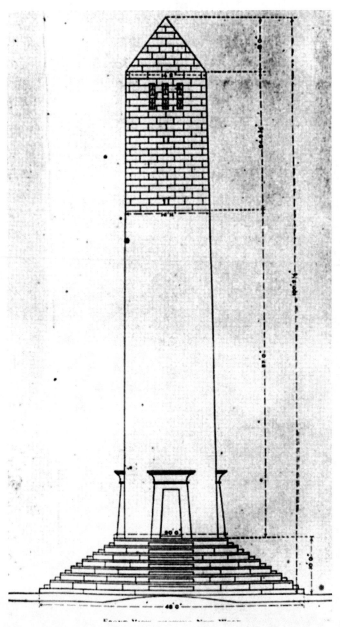

Front View, showing new work.

From a drawing by Alfred F. Theard,
Engineer in charge (1907).

The monument's most characteristic Egyptian ornaments are its four doorways, each with its cavetto cornice and splayed jambs. Three of the doorways, like some of their Egyptian counterparts, are "false doors," and only one frames a true door, the entrance to the spiral stairway.

View showing scaffolding and boiler for the steam hoist, made during the construction of the upper part of the monument. (1908).

Victor Huber, the contractor, (far right, seated) and his crew of marble cutters and setters who put the marble facing on the upper part of the monument. (1908).

The iron steps on the interior were brought to the top of the observatory chamber, which was lined with panels of Georgia marble. At the top there are twelve bronze grilled openings with glazed sash. The entrance is closed by a heavy bronze door (almost inoperative today) and a bronze tablet placed inside the monument is inscribed:

> Monument to the memory of the American soldiers who fell in the Battle of New Orleans at Chalmette, Louisiana, January 8th, 1815. Work begun in 1855 by Jackson Monument Association. Monument placed in custody of United States Daughters of 1776 and 1812 on June 14, 1894. Monument and grounds ceded unto the United States of America by the State of Louisiana on May 24, 1907.
>
> Completed in 1908 under the provisions of an Act of Congress approved March 4th, 1907.

Chalmette Monument framed by moss-hung hackberry trees.

The total cost of the erection of the Chalmette monument, using documented figures was $61,314.00 plus the cost of the land ($5,000.00).

Paid to contractors to Feb. 20, 1856 .... $	9,161.00
Money remaining after completion of Jackson Square statue and used for Chalmette monument	12,153.00
State appropriation of 1857	15,000.00
	$ 36,314.00
Federal appropriation of 1907 to complete monument..........................	25,000.00
Total Cost .... $	61,314.00

Marie Josephine Cruzat de Verges
1890 - 1980

Mrs. de Verges was the great, great granddaughter of Antoine Cruzat and Victoire de Lino de Chalmet, whose family's plantation comprised part of the battlefield of the Battle of New Orleans. She was a founder and longtime president of the Chalmette National Historical Park Association, a group which strives to keep alive the historical significance of the battlefield and its monument.

By the end of the year 1908, the work was completed and accepted by the War Department. On March 16, 1909, Col. Beach, United States Engineers, under whose supervision the final work on the monument had been completed, in ceremonies at the site, highly complimented the patriotic women of the United States Daughters of 1776 and 1812 for their efforts and presented their president, Mrs. Victor Meyer with the keys to the monument and officially returned the memorial to their care.

In November, 1929, the Daughters informed the Secretary of War that they could continue the upkeep no longer.

On December 12, 1929, Congressman James O'Connor introduced a bill in Congress with a view to the establishment of a national park [of the Chalmette Battlefield]. The measure providing for the transfer of the monument to the War Department was approved by the President . . .

In June, 1930 the ceremony of the transfer of the custody of the monument took place at the base of the spire, ending the 36-year guardianship of this group of public-spirited women. [1]

On August 10, 1939, Chalmette was designated a national historical park and from that time on, has been the ward of the National Park Service.

Since its founding on January 9, 1949 the Chalmette National Historical Park Association has been active as an auxiliary organization. Its objects are "to assist the National Park Service to enlarge, develop, maintain and interpret the Park as a suitable memorial to the great historical event which occurred there in 1814-1815."

---

[1] On January 24, 1930, the organization's title was changed to United States Daughters of 1812—Chalmette Chapter.

Chalmette Monument showing damage caused by a stroke of lightning.

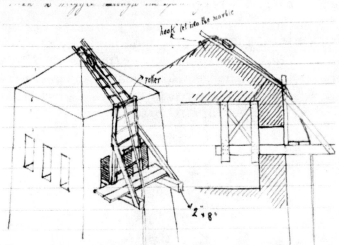

According to the leaders of the Daughters of 1776 and 1812, the monument was struck by lightning three times. In 1921, repairs had to be made to the tip of the pyramidal summit which had been damaged by a bolt. How to get the 200-pound piece of marble and the man to put it in place without building a hundred-foot scaffold was the difficulty. Albert Weiblen, a well-known monument dealer, solved the problem by building an ingenious self-supporting scaffold thrust through two of the little windows of the observation room. A sketch of the scaffold, the ladder to climb to the top and rig to haul up the stone has been preserved and is illustrated. A lightning rod was installed to end further trouble.

Bibliography

Louisiana, Legislature. *Report of the Jackson Monument Association.* New Orleans: 1855.

Louisiana, Legislature. *Report of the Commissioners of the Jackson Association.* Baton Rouge: 1856.

United States Daughters of 1776 and 1812. *Minute books 1893-1974 and Scrapbooks, 1896-1974.*

Theard, Alfred F. *Work of Completing the Chalmette Monument.* Association of Engineering Societies (Bulletin), Vol. XLIII, No. 3, (Plans) *Monument to the Memory of American Soldiers, Battle of New Orleans At Chalmette, La.* Sheets Nos. 1 to 4, Present Chalmette Plan, Elevation and Sections. Drawn under the direction of Capt. Mc Indoc by Alfred F. Theard, Civil Eng. and Architect, August, 1907.

Bull, Mrs. Anna Lewis. *Facts About The Chalmette Monument and Its Caretakers, The Louisiana Society United States Daughters 1776-1812.* ND, NP. (Ca. 1930).

Roush, J. Fred. *Chalmette National Park.* National Park Service, Washington, D.C.: 1958, reprinted 1961.

National Park Service. *Chalmette National Historic Park.* (Visitors Pamphlet). (Ca. 1980's).

Huber, Leonard V. *Jackson Square Through the Years.* The Friends of the Cabildo, New Orleans, La.: 1982.

Kernion, George C. H. *Address on November 16, 1933 at the dedication of a bronze plaque in honor of Felicite Toutant Beauregard Gayoso de Lemos Tennent,* Howard-Tilton Memorial Library.

de Verges, Marie Cruzat. *A Brief History of the United States Daughters of 1776-1812 and Chalmette Chapter.* (1942) 11 pp. typescript, Howard-Tilton Memorial Library, Tulane University.

New Orleans Notarial Archives.
New Orleans. *La Courrier de la Louisiane.*
New Orleans. *The Daily Picayune.*
New Orleans. *New Orleans Republican.*
New Orleans. *Daily True Delta.*
New Orleans. *The Times-Picayune.*

Acknowledgments

The author is greatly indebted to Miss Rose Lambert, Head Librarian of the Center for Louisiana History and to Miss Florence M. Jumonville, Head of the library of the Historic New Orleans Collection, for furnishing copies of original documents and other source material; to Collin B. Hamer, Jr., Head of the Louisiana Division of the New Orleans Public Library and members of his department for courtesies shown; to Wilbur E. Meneray, Head of Manuscripts and Special Collections, Howard-Tilton Memorial Library, Tulane University for the use of important source material; to Wilson A. Greene, Park Manager of the Chalmette National Historic Park for the loan of plans and photo-graphs; to Bruns D. Redmond for his help and the loan of a photograph from his collection; to Samuel Wilson, Jr., F.A.I.A. for the loan of items from his collection and for reading the text critically; to Henri A. Gandolfo for the gift of sketches and to Kendra Comiskey for typing. All have my sincere thanks.

Funds for the publication of the first edition of this booklet were provided from the Venetia and Louis Torre Memorial Fund of the Louisiana Landmarks Society.

About the Author

Leonard V. Huber, New Orleans businessman, historian, lecturer and collector of Louisiana memorabilia has written more than 20 books relating to his native city and state. His best known works are: *New Orleans, A Pictorial History,* published by Crown (New York, 1971) and Louisiana, *A Pictorial History,* published by Scribners (New York, 1975).

The Louisiana Landmarks Society

The Louisiana Landmarks Society was established in 1950. However, its historic preservation advocacy activities began at the start of 1949 when members of the formative New Orleans chapter of the Society of Architectural Historians (an outgrowth of a history of Louisiana architecture course taught at Tulane University by Samuel Wilson, Jr.) banded together to save an early-nineteenth-century colonial Creole plantation, called the David Olivier House, from demolition. Leading the charge to preserve Gallier Hall in the 1950s and defeat the proposed Riverfront Expressway in the 1960s, Landmarks rapidly defined preservation advocacy in New Orleans. The current mission of the Louisiana Landmarks Society, the city and state's first historic preservation organization, is to promote historic preservation through education, advocacy, and operation of the Pitot House.

The values of the Louisiana Landmarks Society are manifested in the Pitot House, the nonprofit organization's home since 1964. This rare surviving example of colonial-era Creole architecture provides Landmarks with a site for exhibitions and educational programming that promote its preservation message. The historic structure and its interpreted grounds provide a transformative historic house tour experience for local and out-of-town visitors and provide the local public with a historically authentic and aesthetically idyllic setting for private functions.

The Louisiana Landmarks Society's major programs include an annual series of free public lectures on preservation topics, award recognition for outstanding preservation efforts, and the presentation of New Orleans' Nine Most Endangered properties—a program modeled after the National Trust for Historic Preservation's Eleven Most Endangered program.

In 1987, the board of trustees of the Louisiana Landmarks Society established a publication fund, named in honor of Samuel Wilson, Jr. The object of Landmarks' publication activity is to foster a more general interest in the architectural tradition of the region and to encourage publication of regional architectural history research. In the years since, Landmarks has published and marketed numerous monographs on architecture and preservation topics. By 2010, efforts to expand Landmarks' publishing program resulted in the creation of a publishing and distribution partnership with Pelican Publishing Company. Landmarks' share of proceeds from this partnership will support perpetuation of the Samuel Wilson, Jr. Publication Fund and its mission to provide for the development of future Louisiana Landmarks Society publications.

CPSIA information can be obtained at www.ICGtesting.com
Printed in the USA
LVOW062038091211

258715LV00001B/1/P